RED ROAD

CLAN MOTHER
SHORAN WAUPATUKUAY PIPER

RED ROAD

Content: Clan Mother Shoran Waupatukuay Piper & Queen Co. Meadows, the Hoodoo Queen
Cover/Art Design: Conjure South Publications
Editors: Sasha Ravae

Published by:
Conjure South Publications
P.O. Box 404
Mobile, AL 36601
www.conjuresouth.com

TABLE OF CONTENTS

ANCESTRAL REVERENCE

Saygo! Thank you to all my honorable ancestors, known and unknown. My father Chief Big Eagle, tribal leader/medicine man; Tom Flanders, tribal spiritual advisor/medicine man; my grandmother Clan Mother/Chieftess Rising Star, tribal leader/medicine woman; my great-grandfather George Sherman; Roy Black Bear, medicine man; and Mary and Eliza Freeman, who were African American Indians of the Paugussett Nation, free slaves who had a haven on our tribal nation's land for all the enslaved who had escaped.

Thank you for the life you have given me to live every day, walking in your moccasins. The teachings the lessons and the blessings, I'm so grateful to have been guided by you all. Thank you for your sacrifice, blood, sweat and tears, and for always being around me, helping me, protecting me, showing me...but most of all, for guiding the pen in my hand to paper for my writings. I hear your every word with love and grace. Aho oneha.

ACKNOWLEDGMENT & APPRECIATION

Thank you, my ancestors, for your prayers and teachings. You surround me daily, so I thank you for your divine guidance and supreme protection.

Thank you to my family and very close friends for your support and encouragement. To Queen Co. Meadows, the Hoodoo Queen, my longtime dear friend who I've known and worked with for many many moons, I'm thankful for the opportunity to be writing this book and publishing it with Conjure South Publications. I look forward to continuing our friendship and workings together for many more moons to come.

Much love, and many blessings.

TERMINOLOGY

Aho: Thank you. Amen. Agree. Yes.
Bear: Makwa/Machk
Chanupa: Sacred pipe
Creator: Great mystery, universe, creator of all living things, beings; term used in ceremony.
Father Sky: All that's needed to provide for us to live
Grandmother Moon: Female energy, controls the waters, controls the women's cleansing moon cycle
Inipi: Sweat lodge
Kinnickinnick: Tobacco
Many Moons: Years, a long time
Oneha: Till we meet again
Red Road: Right path of life
Regalia: Not a costume. special traditional material, symbols, culturally specific.
Reservation: Legal land, home for American Indians, documented on maps, Bureau of Indian affairs, state
Saygo: Greetings
Sky World/Sky People: Spirits, heavens, stars, those who came before us
Tradish: Traditional

OPENING PRAYER

All of my honorable ancestors, known and unknown, and Mother Earth, may I be your vessel and walk in your path of footsteps with peace and beauty on your sacred land that you once walked with pride, honor and respect. Aho

CHAPTER 1
Connecting to the Red Road

By walking the red road in your life, walking on the path with the spiritually inclined, you will find balance.

Red is the color that spirits see for tribes. This sacred color also represents that of the warriors, victory, and courage. It's also about being connected and respectful to all my relations, Mother Earth and Father Sky, and healing traditions and concepts. (Please, read the terminology section, and you will understand the meanings of such words.)

Being on the red road means being grounded and balanced spiritually, physically, mentally, and emotionally. To put your bare feet into the grass/ground and take deep breaths as you feel Mother Earth between your toes. This technique is something you can do daily and/or on stressful days.

This is hard for someone who has lost their way and has fallen off their path. Those who have lost their connection will not survive in *some* or *all* of these areas of the red road. It's our prophecy to survive…we have, and we will.

We live *with* Mother Earth. Earth doesn't belong to us; we belong to the earth.

What Makes Me Indigenous?

I was born an American Indian, raised as an American Indian, live and still continue to live as an American Indian, and I will die an American Indian.

Since the day I was born, being raised at my father's knee taught me the ways of the American Indian and how to live for tribal and cultural survival, to preserve the arts and crafts that are real, authentic, and handmade by our tribe and other tribes, and to preserve the culture and traditions, to defend and protect ancient property, rights, and lands.

I walk the path of my ancestors daily, with my ancestors by my side. My father, Chief Big Eagle told me over and over again, and then again that "if you don't follow the American Indian ways of life, it will come back to haunt you."

Reclaiming our ancestral home, he said with his voice raised, "I'm not like the old Indians." Refusing to move "camp" aka reservations rather than face up to the white man, he said, "I'll die and go to hell right here."

You better believe it. I am my father's daughter, and I'm a hundred times worse.

This is a prayer my father would say now and then that would give him strength and help him to be patient in telling his stories; I now say this at times:

"Believe that you are a child of the creator, that you were born pure, with a goodness and strength that all his children are born with. Believe that, if you have strayed from the teachings of your elders, you are not lost. Readjust your ways, and the creator will give you the vision and power to believe in yourself. Acknowledge the creator through thanksgiving and prayer, for the strength to do what is right. Ask the elders for counseling to guide your life back to the wisdom of our old ways. Be not discouraged. Make your life calm and rewarding. Find peace and acquire serenity. Believe that, with the creator's help, you can regain control."

When you're born, you're put on a tribal roll. It confirms your status with Indian Affairs, and you are recognized as *Indigenous.* You have to go through these legalities. You have to have these governmental statements and permits to be an indigenous individual. To take that step to be legally recognized, you have to contact the tribal office and have documents that shows that your lineage is connected to that family—birth certificates, old Indian cards, Tribal ID cards, etc.

When it comes to identifying as a legal American Indian, you have to look at your genealogy. You may be looking at documents, and those documents may not say that you're Native. It may read *black* or *mulatto,* but with these documents, if they read these things, you can still find out.

It will be connected to the files that they have on record, and it will give one side of the family. It will show who's connected with who. Anyone looking to go about this legally, your documents may not read *Indian* or *Native.* This doesn't exclude you.

Once you present this information, you can legally be recognized. They don't even accept DNA anymore. It has to go down the lineage.

Say you're struggling to find the information, you may say, "Will a tribe or nation recognize me without this?" Yes, a couple of tribes will do dual membership. It's where one tribe takes in another American Indian into their tribe, so a person who claims, but does not have the legal documentation, can be adopted into the tribe.

On TikTok, people are talking about the percentage of being Native. There are some tribes, people within, that have a very conservative view of who is native, and who is not. In the past, you had to be a quarter to be considered Indian.

One may struggle to identify as an American Indian; people may be fearful to connect, because they may think, "I'm not a particular percentage or look a certain type of way."

I would say to those people: you know who you are. You know where you come from. Stay on that path and stay in your ways. The creator made everybody's features. If you are a person of indigenous descent, you have some proof, and the tribe or nation that you feel strongly about doesn't welcome you, firstly, you didn't choose the blood in your body, so you shouldn't be judged. Continue to connect to your path as an American Indian to the best of your ability.

You may find someone who is legally and completely recognized that says, "Yes, you are my brother/sister. We are children of the creator, and I recognize you as one of us." That may be all you need.

No piece of paper can validate your blood.

Just because you can't link it back, doesn't mean you're not. If the community recognizes you, you're in, no matter what anyone says, feels, or thinks.

You may find a tribe/clan that may not be your own, but it can say, "We recognize you; we see you."

Life on the Reservation

Living on the reservation as I have all my life, you learn to live off the land. Your ancestors love people who work the land, which gives you even more reason to do right by it.

My family was *very* powerful and gifted, owned horses and gardens, and they worked the land like no tomorrow. Most of the fruits and vegetables, especially the medicines that are produced, stocked, and shelved, came from my ancestors *before* Columbus arrived. My ancestors also made medicines from over 200 plants straight from the land and used every bit of it—the roots and leaves to develop cures for wounds, sores, and illnesses of all kinds.

They planted corn in certain colors, because corn represents protection, and all the blessings that the creator gave us. There are certain colors—earth tones, purple, and blue—that are used for cooking, baking, and spiritual doings, before putting it into medicine pouches and special colored cloths, or making it into jewelry to wear. Not everyone can wear a corn necklace or bracelet. Not even everyone in my tribe wears one.

Wearing one means that a certain ancestor that works with that corn wants you to wear it. The corn is not for you. Corn is a particular spirit that connects us to multiple aspects, to multiple spirits of the land, earth, ancestors, and these spirits align with colors, the season, and that space.

In this book, we cannot specify what particular color is connected to which spirit, because it's not a novelty and can't be sold.

Whether it's corn, or another animal, fruit, or herb, these spirits are used from the "roota to the toota". We use *all* pieces. This may be through making jewelry, a doll, or smoking, for example. When you are on the reservation, on the earth, nothing is taken without it being given back.

We do many of these things on a daily basis, as in *we* feed the land and care for it, along with the wildlife. We care for the ancestors' spaces and gravesites, and spirit animals through space cleansings and protection barriers. We will also, if needed, or as the time comes, smoke any dark energy clear out.

On the reservation, there are a lot of alcohol and drugs present. The youth feels like there's no hope. They feel like they are hit for being afro-indigenous, or just indigenous. And, although, there are antidotes, the problem is getting those who are addicted to take them, but they usually O.D.

My father, on our reservation, took out an eagle's feather, put it on this person's shoulder, they started to convulse, and he pulled the drugs from out of their body.

When they woke up, they were clean.

With access to our medicine men and women, there are ways to fix this situation, but people are unwilling to get the help they need. It's usually a one and done, or they keep coming back, but substance abuse is still a huge pandemic on all reservations.

There was another person who came to my father one night with an alcohol problem. He was angry, agitated, talking crap, and everybody was there, but we just had to ignore him. The bad spirits were being pulled out.

It worked for a while, and then something bad happened in his life, and he fell off the wagon again. My father told him that he was going to die soon...and he did.

Alcohol spirits are herbal spirits, so it's important to understand that they don't work with everybody the same. They especially don't work with indigenous people in that way.

The man had done something bad in his past, and my father knew. But, you cannot continue to talk about that; you can't keep bringing up the past, because it gives those negative spirits energy and fire, so that bad things continue to come.

It's so important to understand that by dismissing them, this only elevated these negative and detrimental spirits in this particular individual.

All of his spiritual items, he had desecrated. He was mixing liquor, so he didn't have a preference. He would drink whatever.

Alcoholic drinks are used in our tradition, but you have to know how to control it. You're not supposed to be using it just to be using it.

Through ceremonies, the reservation is a space of healing. Like walking through a cemetery, it's spiritualized. The land is sacred and holds so many blessings for our people. You have to see it, feel it, hear it...*everything*.

When you come onto the reservation, live on it, it is undeniable that you feel the sacred spirit, the Great Spirit. When you eat the foods, you can taste the sacredness of this space. Every sense of your human body experiences the greatness of this sacred space.

Living on the reservation connects us beyond our imagination...it forces us to go back to the land, back to the earth.

The majority of the old one's are gone with the Great Spirit. They have passed the traditions down to our generation to continue onto the next seven to come. You have to keep these traditions going daily on the reservation and in your life, so you don't lose sight of who you are and where you come from. The reservation is our identity. Without it, we're nothing and don't exist to the government. My responsibility as Clan Mother is to protect my ancestors and preserve the culture the best I can.

How does a native, indigenous, afro-indigenous American feel on the land? Being on the reservation feels peaceful, like *this is where I'm supposed to be at.*

Of course, we want to process improve, but you can feel the spirits all around you. It's a good feeling to live off the land.

Ceremonies

When it comes to ceremonies, we do them on a weekly/monthly basis. Living on the reservation, there are a lot of ceremonies you can do alone, or with a group. Everything is usually done in a circle.

Our youth, they are either picked for fire keeping, digging holes, or just sitting silent. From carrying the rocks, they would have to go to the water and add the prayer ties—whatever the elders call them to do.

Children are brought in on ceremonies for a number of reasons—to sit still and just listen, or they may stay up until 2 a.m. to watch the fire or watch over the women at night. What you will also find not only in this tradition, but in African American culture as well, is the importance of children. (I am not just native to this land. I am also African American.)

Through taking Queen Co. Meadows' *Superstitions & Folklore* Class, something that didn't surprise me, but was quite interesting, was the same way that a child is pure in our tradition is the same way it is within African American culture. Which is why you would have a child sweep or clean the yard.

In traditional spaces, we understand the importance of a child, their energy, asè, purpose, and gifts, and it's very important because you may find this in other cultures as well. Many people don't understand how powerful a child can be due to their purity. Because they have not been polluted, they are able to see things clearer. Their world is the spiritual world. People call it *imagination,* but the truth is that a child is closer to the other side than a middle-aged person is.

In western society, we try to quiet a child and give them a bunch of rules. When it should be, "Let me teach you about life through the earth...your hands are much sweeter than mine."

Black Natives in the U.S.

Since the time of creation, we all know that the creator made all our features, including skin color. American Indians and African Americans were either called "Black Indians" or "Black Native Americans".

Truthfully, the slave trade affected both Native Americans and Africans; they were both combined at one point. They had different relations, and intermarriage took place upon survival. American Indians blended with the African Americans and were occasionally kidnapped into slavery.

It's important to note that *97% of African Americans are American Indians.* The color of our skin, and in the majority of tribes, hair texture, our looks were how we were all identified—either *black* or *American Indian,* or should I say, they labeled us as *negro.*

In our tribes, we have documents that says who is American Indian & Black, or just American Indian, or just *negro* (literally, that word was used). It also states who married who, and who was born to who.

My mother was labeled *Chinese* on one of my brother's birth certificates, because of her eye-shape and long, dark-brown hair.

This was a false label for my mother, as she was far from Chinese.

I, myself, have been identified as *Puerto Rican* and *Black Indian,* and one time, I was even called a *prairie nigg*—I won't spell the rest of the word, as it's derogatory. But, you understand what I am saying…

At that very second, I asked, "What does that even mean…?"

Yes, of course, common sense kicked in…obviously, I knew what it meant, but that was the first time it had been directed at me personally.

I then heard that same word in a movie one time; acting or not, just *wow*. Who comes up with these words?

The Trail of Tears

During the *Trail of Tears,* the government forced Native Americans by gunpoint from their homelands to walk hundreds of miles to other government-made camps/reservations. It was called the *Indian Removal Act.*

Thousands died from disease, warfare, murder…and so on. A lot of them became angry and lost, and even became slave owners themselves. The government said that it was "ethnic cleansing" and "the only good Indian was a dead Indian." These tribes who were on the *Trail of Tears,* after enduring being on the chain gang, are the Cherokee, Choctaws, Chickasaw, Creek, and Seminoles. There was so much pain and suffering during this time.

The tribal regions of over 500 tribes worldwide are: Eastern Woodlands, the Great Plains, Southeast, Southwest, Inuit, Western, Midwest, and the Northern Woodlands. Tribal clans and spirit animals that are associated with clans provide medicine, food, protection, leadership, teachings, and learning.

In tribes, small groups were called "clans" that shared the family's bloodline, or ancestral lineage. They would have their own symbol and/or spirit.

All tribes worldwide, clan names are animals. These animals are Turtle, Crow, Bear, Deer, Wolf, Eagle, and many more, as there are over 500 tribes, as I mentioned.

It's very important to understand the history passed down from generation-to-generation. My tribal clan is the Black Bear clan with 150 tribal blood enrolled members. We are guardians of the community and protectors and carry the medicine and strength and courage; we are powerful and can be very feisty. We are strong, fearless, wise authority figures, medicine people, and noble spirits; we are leaders who are feared, but also admired and respected.

We don't eat bear, as you don't eat where you come from. We can have and use their teeth, fur, claws, full body, or just the head. We make blankets from their fur and bear grease/oil, which is used for baking, your hair, and your skin. (It has no stinky scent.) But, we can never *eat* bear—nothing of the bear, no bear jerky…nothing. That's like eating your mother.

The majority of tribes all over the world have African American/American Indians. We, as in African Americans and American Indians, have shared history—the violence and trauma of being enslaved, colonized, and separated. We are the *non*-privileged. We have endured the harassment and discrimination that we faced because of our color and ethnicity.

My ancestors were dark-skinned with dark hair and dark eyes. That is how the creator made us. We all must return to a spiritual way of life—the way of all of our ancestors. That is how we are all going to make it through these tough times.

Yes, there are struggles on the reservation, as there are all over the United States. People are dealing with identity, racism, murder, and the disappearance of indigenous women, men, and children, especially our women.

Unfortunately, the human trafficking rate is very high, and our impoverished areas are at the government's hands. Nobody hears us in those governmental departments, or the political parties who play both sides of the fence. All they do is take and take from all of the tribes; it's not all casinos.

As a Black native, you have to get your kids on the rolls, so that you are able to receive a Tribal ID Card.

By the time you're born, you're already dealing with the government. Our Tribal ID, it's like having a Driver's License or State ID. We used to be able to use it everywhere, except it was for our own tribe. The state in which you live provided them, but now the tribes must provide them. We can no longer use them as a state ID; they're used for things like schooling, or when you're on another reservation. It comes in handy for some things, but Tribal leaders still call ahead of time to let people know that they're coming.

Tribes had their own license plates too, but as soon as they left the reservation, they couldn't use them anymore.

If you have a reservation, you have certain contracts with the state, and they take care of their half. But, they only do certain things, so it's up to the tribe to make things better for their people.

The Medicine Wheel

The Medicine Wheel is a sacred spiritual hoop used for health and healing. The four directions are the East, West, North, and South. Father Sky, Mother Earth, and Spirit Trees all symbolize cycles of life.

- *The four colors of the Medicine Wheel are:* black, yellow, red, and white, which represents the human races.

- *The four main medicines are:* tobacco, white sage (some may use Lakota sage), cedar, and sweetgrass.

The Medicine Wheel can take different forms, and the ceremony movement is in a circular, clockwise motion. Everything is done in a circular motion, clockwise, that is.

The Medicine Wheel represents seasons, life stages and aspects, the elements of nature, animals, and ceremonial plants.

It can be used in ceremonies with feathers added and can also be used in your daily life. In different parts of the regions that I mentioned, some tribes have similarities and differences of how they do things, including the Medicine Wheel (the color order may differ).

Black
Represents: Sage, Fall, Moon, West, Water, Wolf, Coyote, Bear, Adult-Parents

Yellow
Represents: Tobacco, East, Spring, Fire, Eagle, Sun, Birth, Childhood

Red
Represents: Sweetgrass, South, Protection, Summer, Earth, Buffalo, Sage, Mouse, Coyote, Earth-Bodies, Youth, and Adolescents

White
Represents: Cedar, Air, Wind, North, Winter, Buffalo, Bear, Stars, Death, Elders, Grandparents

On the Wheel, there are:

- Four races of humankind living together in harmony

- Four sacred plants
- Four directions offering its own lessons
- Four wind spirit animals
- Four seasons, 4x of the day
- Seasons of the year, and the seasons of your life

CHAPTER 2
The Traditional Chain-of-Command

The importance of a chain-of-command is to have a voice to speak for everybody. You need someone to go to the government on your behalf, a voice to show you your spiritual ways and tend to the land. If there's no council leader, there's no tribe.

If you don't have someone living on the reservation, the government can come revoke your reservation's status, because there are no tribal leaders to speak about your needs and wants.

It's very important to the reservation that the chain-of-command governs the reservation, that they are the voice outside of the reservation.

Tribal leaders, clan mothers, chiefs all have the same blood lineage. They are looked at for many years by the tribal leader and medicine men and women, but they look upon you, and they choose you. For the council and secretary, these positions are chosen through elections, and there are appointments. You are on that seat or board from 2-4 years.

Tribes have a chain-of-command that consists of:

- Clan Mother
- Tribal Leader (whose position is higher than the Chief's and Chieftess')
- Chief/Co-Chief
- War/Peace Chief (and/or Council Chief)
- Tribal Chairman

Not every tribe will have all of these chain-of-commands in place. It could be the tribal leader, council/chairman, war chief and/or peace chief.

The Importance of the Chain of Command Roles

Clan mothers are female, chiefs can be unisex, with the chieftess being female as well. In our tribe, the co-chief and war chief have always been male. A tribe's spiritual advisor and medicine man/women are unisex.

A traditional chief would be tribal leader if no clan mother is selected. In the absence of a clan mother, a council of elders (tribal members) shall select a chief. The chief is a symbol of unity and permanence, and they choose who is to be next after them, again, if there is no clan mother. If there is a clan mother, the chief can go to her with whomever their appointing and tell the clan mother and then it's her decision. A son or a daughter can be chosen who is trustworthy, has good character, and is honest and respectful. They must know how to be Chief and the *do's* and *don'ts,* how to handle and manage their own affairs, and support their own family in order to prove themselves. They are to be faithful to tribal family and serve the tribe till death, or until their too elderly and need to retire from the position or be dehorned, (as in fired or having their title pulled by the clan mother or council if there is no clan mother). All these positions are also done through ceremony; you don't just get a title or name and be on your way. *Please note:* The description of those ceremonies are private tribal matters.

The appearance of the chief includes American Indian jewelry, jeans, and dress shoes or cowboy boots, if able; a cowboy hat and a ribbon shirt, and/or shirts and jackets with tribal logos, patches, prints, and Native sayings. Long hair is always braided or tied back.

The co-chief can have some duties and powers from the traditional chief. Some duties and requirements of the tradish Chief goes for co/council chief as well.

Council Chief can be a son, daughter, sister, brother, parent, or grandchild of the tradish Chief.

My grandmother who was Clan Mother/Chieftess wore her regalia and moccasins daily, even on the transit bus through towns visiting tribal family members. Regalia is made of buckskin or elk skin, and has beads and shells sewn onto the regalia, and it's made with prayers, medicines, blessings, and good intentions. We cannot make medicines, regalia, or crafts if we're sick, tired, or having a bad day, as it will go into the items, and that would be a bad thing for the wearer. Same with moccasins as well, all made from animal hide and some have beaded work onto them. Everything we make is all handmade including some beads from shells; it can take up to six-hours to make one bead.

Nowadays, people think you have to walk around with a headdress, red face paint, and have long black hair in order to be identified as American Indian. If your skin is dark, and your hair is of African American texture, you're identified as *black*. We know who we are and where we come from, and we don't need to show it by dressing a certain way, walking a certain way, and so on. But because people think the last American Indian died in an old cowboy and Indian film, and all African Americans were killed off in slave times, we now, as a daily routine, need to show them different, that we are still here—proud descendant people of our ancestors—and that we're not going anywhere.

Life as Clan Mother

I was looked upon in grammar school when I was about 8 or 9 by my grandmother who was the Chieftess/Clan Mother, Tribal Leader, at the time, and it was told to my father who was appointed Tribal Hereditary Chief, Tribal Leader, by my grandmother. It was documented in the Indian Affairs Department in the state that my reservation resides, and in Washington D.C..

The gentleman who I have become great friends with, who has since retired from Indian Affairs, still remembers to this day the papers in his hand being brought to all the proper people for signatures

In 2008, my father died. As American Indians, we know when we are going to go. So, I was appointed, had my ceremony, and then my father passed.

As clan mother, you have good days, bad days, and everything in-between. Your plate is always full, because everyone always needs something. Taking care of your own home becomes that much harder, because you have to work for your people. You have to be there spiritually, be able to answer state needs, there's always something that needs to be signed, or someone may need permission for this event or this powwow. It's truly 24/7.

I have taken breaks, but that doesn't work. Even if I let everyone know that I'm out-of-town, they will still text me.

I currently have three emails and two phone numbers. Of course, it helps to have a secretary and assistant, but not everything can be done for you.

But, as much work as it is, I've been honored and thankful from the moment that I was appointed. I'm happy about where I've gotten my people. I was able to make changes that my family didn't have the opportunity to make.

Clan Mother is a title that should not be challenged. Just because you *claim* that you are a clan mother, because you *claim* that you are an indigenous American Indian doesn't mean that you can claim this title due to your own personal feelings and thoughts.

There has to be a ceremony with witnesses, documentation, and signatures. This is also a legal, governmental title. I am *legally* known as *Clan Mother.*

In the space of appropriation, not many people know it, but we understand that once something is mentioned in a public space, it can never be taken back. If you want to appropriate with the sage, have your hand at that, but even there...you're playing on a very fine line. But, to misuse and abuse this title, you are risking having warriors at your front door, and being banned from every reservation across the land. It's like having a warrant.

The news will fly so fast through native country, not to mention, our way of doing witchcraft; someone's going to get that process going on you. You'll be really embarrassed...it gets ugly; I've seen people fall off the face of the earth.

When it comes to being a clan mother, you are literally mother to all. Yes, you may have your personal family, and you are "Mama," but you are "Mother" to everyone else. When you have this title, it's like any king, queen, or priest/priestess, if you are holding that crown, you have to hold those responsibilities. You *personally* can't claim to be a clan mother; you are chosen.

If someone is claiming *clan father* or *clan papa,* we all know that this is a fraud. But, there are secret codes that are used between all clan mothers. There are secret exchanges and handshakes, for example, so if you claim to be a clan mother, and you don't know them, you will endure the wrath of the spirits and the community.

Are there some clans that don't have clan mothers?

Yes, there are some tribes that don't have clan mothers, or a hereditary chief.

My father was having visions that were told to everyone about me becoming Clan Mother before it happened. Once you're 30, you can then take that step, but it's dependent on the prior Clan Mother stepping down. Right now, documents have been written up about who will be the next clan mother in my tribe; it's a secret, so I can't say who.

As a clan mother, you're the overseer of the family/tribal nation. In this traditional role, as the matriarch, you're looked upon by previous leaders who decide who the next leader is going to be. You definitely have to meet the criteria and go through a ceremony.

Clan Mothers are in charge of appointing tribal chiefs and other positions, and have the tie-breaker and last vote/say so. We are caretakers and life givers. We are responsible for ceremonies, rituals, funerals, weddings, and the teaching of history, as well as the medicines and spirituality. We are the decision-makers and healers…and so much more.

Clan Mothers are the tribal leaders; we advise the tribe on tribal customs, history, genealogy, and spiritual guidance. We confer titles and other honorary distinctions on tribal members. We are the traditional role, the matriarchal woman.

In our daily lives, we wear our sacred spiritual and native jewelry. Our clothing is of regular clothing that may consist of American Indian sayings, pictures or prints on our shirts and coats. We may even wear our ribbon skirts and/or ribbon shirts. Our hair may even be braided and/or let down to hang. We wear beaded belts to hold up our pants, or use belts made with shells.

The Tribal Council

The selection of the tribal council is all about seeing if someone can take care of the tribe. It's different than being a clan mother. They have to be able to take care of their own family, first and foremost. Co-Chiefs work with the War/Peace Chief and Tribal Council/Chairman. They do a lot of political work.

You are chosen as an adult, not as a child. This is different, because you have proven that you are nurturing, diplomatic, and responsible, and this shows that you can be a traditional Chief.

Peace/War Chief

What is a war/peace chief? It's your own sovereignty court; if the family is having disagreements, a peace chief helps to keep the peace. A war chief is a little bit of the same thing, but when it's time to handle something, they handle it.

Warriors

Our warriors are there to protect us, especially the elderly and the ones who can't protect themselves. They do the hunting, and they will get their hands dirty.

In order to be chosen as a warrior, you have to make a sacrifice. My son, who is 13 now, when he was 5-6, we were at a powwow, and this man kept pushing this little girl. The girl's parents couldn't get up because they were working, so this man tried to take her, but my son jumped in and saved her. Now, he's her warrior for life. Every time he sees her, he has to bring her something. There was a ceremony and everything.

Warriors are those who protect the tribal leaders, medicine men/women, tribal families, and children. They sacrifice themselves to care for the elders, and the ones who are defenseless at times.

They also hunt for animal hide to be used for regalia-making and blankets. We hunt wild game and fish for food, in addition to the grocery store foods we eat.

Spiritual Advisors

Let's have the discussion about the *spiritual advisor*, or the *medicine men/women*.

For the record, we don't like or approve of the term *shaman.* Anyone appropriating or claiming to be American Indian and using this is BS. Many out here believe if you don't use this term, you must not be the real thing. But, how do you tell a fish that it's not a fish?

When you step into connecting, not just to the path, but to a culture of people, you have to swallow the pill that is truly given.

This is *not* a term that we use or stand by, so you must do the same.

Maybe, some other tribe on Jupiter, or the natives of the other universes, they may be *shamans,* but when it comes to the American Indians on these lands, we are *spiritual advisors.*

Traditionally, some choose to be called *medicine man/woman,* but everyone has their own term that they use.

I did a Juneteenth parade, and everybody was walking around. One woman went up to one of my warriors wanting to interview me about me being a "shaman," and he said, "I don't think she's going to do the interview about that."

You can't think every American Indian is a *shaman.* That term wasn't even used in our ancestors' time.

A *spiritual advisor* helps with guidance—any type of help or healing. There is no formal training or school to go to. This person is advising you, and they will talk to you. Some of us will give you a story or two and explain next steps for those who seek us out. We don't usually advertise our services; it's all about word-of-mouth.

"By the way, do you know somebody…?"

A lot of people call or email the tribal office. We can always say "no," and don't have to give a reason for it, but we always take in our own.

Within American Indian life, the *spiritual advisor* is similar to your *seer* in traditional African spirituality, or within the African American community. This person knows things, so they may have used stories and fables. This is the person who can give you the tools you need. This would be the person who would do divination. If you're going to a reader who is using tarot, bones, or playing cards, for example, the *spiritual advisor* is the equivalent in the American Indian community that provides this space.

One thing I do love is how Queen Co. brings the clear indication in the African American community that lives in traditional African American spirituality; certain titles like the *conjurer, worker, seer,* or *diviner,* it's very similar in our community.

When you get back to traditional ways of living, there is a natural chain-of-command. Everyone who has a title, knows that they have a title. Those without a title know that their purpose is just different. The more people who can accept this truth, that not everybody in the tribe is a medicine man or woman, war/peace chief, or clan mother, the better. The whole clan respects these titles because they are anointed, chosen, and communally appointed. There is no ego involved, because the tribe understands that these people have abilities they don't have, and that it benefits everyone.

Medicine Man, Medicine Woman

If the *spiritual advisor* is the equivalent of the *seer* or *diviner* in the African American community, as American Indians, you would then assume that the medicine man/woman is the *conjurer.*

A *medicine man/woman* possesses the supernatural and provides healing. This is why the term *shaman* comes up. Shamans hold supernatural power. Medicine men/women wouldn't just heal diseases; they could be a seer or a healer.

As I mentioned, if the *spiritual advisor* is the equivalent to the *diviner*, the *medicine man/woman,* they may hold this position. They are the ones who hold the supernatural abilities to build and heal.

People want to stick with the title of *shaman,* but in reality, just to show you the comparison not just in the American Indian life, or African American life, you will hear, "that child is gifted," supernaturally gifted to see or divine. *Spiritual Advisor* is a title that's not only limited to just herbalism and herbal medicine, but it means that you have the ability to heal; you know the stems to use, the way of the land, the meat to eat, but it does not limit you to just that. You could have the supernatural ability to do other things too. Although, it doesn't limit you, it doesn't grant you supernatural abilities either.

What is medicine?

Medicine can be healing with the hands, shells, drinks, hot teas, plants, roots and herbs from the land and sacred grounds. This can be seen as cooking with the herbs, or creating baths with cedar, for example, for inflammation, or using essential oils. It can be a number of different things.

Before we get into these different workins', we need to define *medicine.* This term can represent the work you are doing, herbs you are using to help heal, many different aspects, but it is an umbrella term, which includes: herbal workings and workings of the divine in general.

Medicine men and women, they send you off on a vision quest for a week, and they'll do a ceremony. You are deep in the woods; they can see you, but you can't see them.

You have to stay awake, or something is left for you while you're sleeping there. When people hear about the vision quest dream world, the *medicine men/women* would cultivate that. They would lead that, because they have the supernatural ability to do so, not the village. They are the magic of our people. You don't appoint yourself.

For a *medicine man/woman,* the same repercussions for falsely claiming to be a clan mother also applies.

If a certain question is asked of you, and you don't know the answer, you will endure the repercussions for posing and appropriating this space and this individual. Everyone needs to understand that you will not be given these secrets. The knowledge you are looking for will not be given to you.

If you are *chosen,* you would have been brought up as a *medicine man/woman* since a child. As an adult, they will not talk to you about this. You can't know this if you are not of this.

Below, I will list a couple of methods that we would use. I will be using *medicine* in a few different ways:

Woman's Medicine Pouch

A woman's medicine bundle represents their healing and protection.

- *Cowry Shells:* provides clarity, protection, and healing…to use for others and for themselves. Can be given as a gift to the water spirits, from you to them.
- Snail Shells
- 4 Main Medicines *(Sage, Cedar, Sweetgrass, & Tobacco)*

Below, we are going to talk about these main medicines:

Sage Leaf

My goddaughter's mother called me and said that her throat was swollen. I told her to use some sage leaf

"Let me make you some inflammation antibiotic," I said, but she insisted on seeing the white man.

Sweetgrass

Sweetgrass braids are placed in our cars to keep positive energy around and for protection.

Each strand, you have to have a total of 27 strands in each bundle. Each braid has to do with the 7 generations that are to come.

Sage, Tobacco, & Corn Meal
Used for divination, good spirits, and positive energy.

I don't like sage, so we put corn meal along with it. Traditionally, some indigenous people don't vibe with just sage, so there's an herbal blend that is used as an incense.

Tobacco can be used as protection in the four corners of your home. I personally love the sweet smell.

We usually go to the elders and burn it for them, or use it in a chanupa, our sacred pipe, to be smoked.

Sage is like medicine for many of our people. It drives out the bad energy and negative influences; you can cleanse yourself or your space with it. It is also used to ward off bad luck.

When you hear the term *smudge,* this is used in the beauty industry; it is not our language. In this particular space, when I say, "smudge a space," I am literally referring to a smudging ceremony. This is a sacred ceremony; this is not what you do when someone has a bad attitude, or to wake your third-eye, so you can decalcify your penal gland. I am speaking specifically to the ceremony, not the new age shaman, Hollywood smudging.

Women

Women are the backbone, healers, and wisdom keepers for all tribal nations. The woman takes care of the children, household, medicine, and is connected to Mother Moon, love, grace, and song. Women hold a high position in this traditional space, because we are more connected to the natural world.

When you reflect, it's beautiful; all the answers of life are in the natural world. So, even a woman's position as leader, you can find that in multiple spaces. Lions in a pride, for example, the lioness is the hunter. They are the nurturers of the cubs. They are the strength of their nation, and literally the male comes around with his big mane, showboating to impress the lioness.

Birds, the females aren't the ones getting the male birds. In nature, it is more matriarchal. In indigenous culture, you see it the same way, and we're talking about the clan mothers. It's starts here, and it ends here. That doesn't mean that the male is inferior. His purpose is just different. He is valued and needed, but when it comes down to being that individual, it's that matriarchal line.

Women lead the healing among the tribes. Inside them are the powers of strength given by Grandmother Moon and Mother Earth. Women sing the songs of strength, love, prayer, and special powers. Our ancestors, our grandmothers prayed for us, saved us, and got us to where we are today.

The elders say to us from birth, it's the women who will lead the healing of our nations. Clan Mothers learn to practice and align with Mother Earth, Father Sky, land, and water. We are to carry ourselves in a sacred way with respect, and to be humble and modest.

Sacred items are given to the women for representation by a prominent elder or *medicine men/women* with instructions for representation within her clan, tribe, and/or womanhood.

Men

The men are hunters and warriors and have some political affairs and some spiritual affairs as well. They protect the tribal families, and they dance the war dances and sneak up dances. They build the Inipi and also can be the pourer in the Inipi and fire keeping. The firekeeper is to keep the fire going, making sure that no one disrespects the fire spirits.

You have to respect the fire as if it's a person, because if you don't, you'll see the bad side of the fire spirit. You can't put certain items in the fire; it's disrespectful, and the fire will no longer be sacred.

Starting the fire is done in a traditional way, and once the fire is going, then the blessing of the fire and spiritual piece is done with the fire and fire pit area. I cannot put into details as for respect of the firekeepers' sacred ways.

The Inipi is our church; it's our medicine and healing, and spirit is present. It's sacred, and tribes all over had to fight to get it back because of non-indigenous/non-tribal nations abusing our Inipi ways that resulted in people dying and being sickened. Inipi is healing, cleansing, purifying, and much more.

These are our rites; they are sacred and private tribal matters.

Two-Spirited Individuals

Two-spirits are male and female, or intersexed, who combine both male and female unique traits. They are experts in so many ways. In tribes, it's called traditional third-gender. They say the *two-spirit* term is only appropriate for native people, so if you don't have a tribe, you can't claim that role.

I have seen and met over the years at native gatherings two-spirited individuals wearing beautiful colors of their choice on their regalia pieces. I have also witnessed disrespect to them by native people, and some even disowned by relatives. I was at a powwow/native gathering, and a female contest dancer won, and there was controversy that she should be placed in the *male* category and not win on the female side. That went on for days and much more was said, but I won't disclose those nasty comments.

I welcome all two-spirited individuals with open-arms. This is imperative because many people of the LGBTQIA+

community may find a safe haven within indigenous culture. Here in America, this is the only culture that speaks about uplifting, that so many people find refuge in that. But we want to talk more about this.

We want to speak about the beautiful nature of being two-spirited, and the ugly truth of not recognizing it.

Like I've mentioned, they are powerful individuals, and they are also very talented. They are spiritually gifted. All of them that I've met, they are born with certain gifts. They're smarter than the scientists at NASA. They know how to put paperwork together. They can cook better than 5-star chefs. They possess unique traits. They bless the tribes with abilities that other tribes may not possess, or possess well.

I met someone who was an American Indian and a two-spirit. I did some ceremony, and they walked up to me. I didn't know they were two-spirited, because I met them as a man initially.

Can they hold roles? Medicine bundles? Can they have the title as Clan Mother?

In certain tribes, I don't know. But, in my tribe, I would accept it and say, "yes". The ancestors, creator, they have blessed us with a third-gender, and they know what's best for us.

Whatever's been placed on the reservation is for the Great Spirit to know. When it comes to being two-spirited, no one has the authority to negate or dishonor this individual since the creator, the elders, and the ancestors have placed them here in this space. Not only do they belong, but they have a purpose. It could be holding one of these positions. It could come about in a vision and has to be respected by all. But understand that we live in America, white man's America, where there is genocide and appropriation, and because of this, a lot of the mentality and ways of thinking have bled into the other tribes, and they don't accept the third-gender. We understand that this is a huge issue, because it displaces the third-gender. If that is the case, this is only weakening us as a tribe or nation, because if that person is supposed to be our saving grace, and they're rejected, we all lose.

A bigger conversation needs to be had at the national level, not just the tribe, but for the people who have gotten away from the tradition. You can't live traditionally and live with this western mentality. You can't have both.

Understand that being a two-spirited individual, not only do you have the ability to fall under these positions, you probably would, because you hold abilities that others may not. Your space is different and precious and proves more of the magnitude of being a part of the third-gender.

Queen Co. has mentioned, if you look across many cultures, the creators are not gender specific. The mysteries of the world come from that nonbinary god or goddess. It is that individual who is seeing more than others. Even if you don't hold a high title, you'll have a more elevated gift, even if it's making the regalia, cooking, or following your purpose. This always comes with more energy, ideas, traits, and resources.

Children

Children are taught from a very young age, basically from the womb, that it all starts with the beat of the drum and song. They are taught the Indian ways of living, which is very important for tribal and cultural survival. They are taught to know the history, tribal dances and their meanings, and the language—no matter how many words or sentences, you continue to speak it to keep it alive and to keep connected to our ancestors.

They are taught how to do beadwork, make regalia, cook our traditional foods, and all about the spirit guides and animals. I get asked a lot, "How do I know my spirit guide animal?" You can have more than one, and spirit animals are embodied form of a spiritual guide. *(Yes, you can have a human guide that's not an animal.)* Watch your dreams and pay attention, see what you're drawn to and connect to the feeling of the animals.

Example: if you're drawn to turtles and constantly see and hear anything and everything turtle, then it's a turtle.

Spirit animals are teachers and messengers and have a personal relationship with the person. We teach the children dream medicine and vision quests and survival, and to love both their land, traditions, and spirituality. It's all spoken and shown to the children.

Respect is one of the values we teach our children. We must preserve that word, as it's no longer used by others. Children are given an item that represents their name at a naming ceremony. A naming ceremony is our way of doing things, just like a baptism in a church is the non-indigenous way. *Please note:* These ceremony details are private tribal matters.

The item that is given at the naming ceremony symbolizes their name and medicine; the item could be a bear claw necklace or fur, a carved knife, or teeth, etc. They can also be given an item that has been passed down from past generations, consisting of a drum or regalia, something spiritual, or a survival tool, etc.

Code of Ethics

The *Code of Ethics* is for the children. Teaching them and continuing to remind them that this is how we utilize this while we're living.

Just like certain religions that have certain commandments that teach you to be your highest self, Odu, these ethics will give you the guideline to be your best self. We have the same, and we teach this from the moment we are born, until we go back to the journey with our creator—cultural survival and tribal survival.

Living in two different worlds, we're born a different breed. Knowing how the non-indigenous world operates, we make sure we know how to carry ourselves in a sacred way. Everything has a spirit, so we're to be respectful with our customs, manners, and morals. We pray at sunrise, driving to work, early in the morning, in the shower, or walking the dog, we are to be tolerant to those who have lost their way.

Our code has survived for many moons, and those who don't care about African Americans and American Indians can never strip us from our spirit, blood, lineage, or our ancestors.

Code of Ethics:

1. Rise with the sun to pray. Pray often and alone. Great Spirit will hear you if you're the only one speaking.
2. Those who are lost on their path, be tolerant towards them. Jealousy, anger, greed, ignorance, and conceit come from a lost soul. Pray that they'll find guidance.
3. Don't allow others to make your path for you. Search for yourself and by yourself. It's your road and yours alone. Others may, and can, walk it *with* you. But only you can walk it *for* yourself. No one else can walk it for you.
4. Treat your guests with consideration. Offer them food and a good bed to rest in. Treat them with respect and honor.
5. Don't take what's not yours, as in from a person, place, thing, or from a culture. It wasn't given or earned, so it's not yours.
6. Respect all things that are from this earth.
7. Honor other's thoughts, wishes, and words; take it into consideration. Never mock, mimic, or interrupt another person. Allow them their personal expression of speaking.

8. Never speak of others in a bad way. The negative energy that you put out into the universe will multiply when it's returned to you.
9. Everyone makes mistakes; all mistakes can be forgiven.
10. Bad thoughts cause illness of the mind, body, and spirit, so practice confidence.
11. Nature isn't *for* us; it's *a part* of us. It's a part of your worldly family.
12. Children are sacred; they're the seeds of our future. Water them with wisdom and life's lessons and put love into their hearts. When they have grown, give them the space to continue.
13. Avoid hurting the hearts of others. The poison of their pain will return to you.
14. Be truthful at all times. Honesty is the test of one's will within the universe.
15. Keep yourself balanced. Your mental-self, spiritual-self, emotional-self, and physical-self are all you need to be strong, pure, and healthy. Workout the body to strengthen the mind. Grow rich in spirit to cure emotional troubles.
16. Make conscious decisions as to who you will be and how you'll react. Be responsible for your own actions.
17. Respect other's privacy and personal space. Don't touch the personal property of other's, especially sacred and religious objects. That's forbidden.
18. Be true to yourself first. You can't nurture and help others if you can't nurture and help yourself.
19. Respect other's religious beliefs. Don't force your beliefs on others.
20. Share your good fortune and charity with others.

CHAPTER 3
The Medicine Bundle

Cowrie shells, seasnail shells, a woman's shell, all represent the goddess and prosperity—a woman's medicine. These shells are used for currency and jewelry, or are worn and sewn onto regalia. They represent: wealth, good luck, and are used for divination, ceremonial purposes, and protection.

Divination in some spiritual regions is the same, but these spaces may have different ways of identifying meanings.

Medicine Pouches

Medicine pouches are to be kept inside your shirt, not out in the open for all to see, touch, or open, because your medicine can be taken away.

There are different items that are put inside for the individual for different reasons and can only be opened by the person it's meant for. If others open it, the medicine and spirit will leave, and the pouch will be no good and will need to be renewed.

Every now and then, you need to cleanse it, due to it collecting what shouldn't be there. You can always open it and add things to it, but don't desecrate it.

Arrowheads/Flints

These items stand for several things, protection being one of them. When an arrow is launched, it flies in a straight path. This also reminds us to stay on the good road in life, and how wandering too far off the path gets us into trouble. For some, it's hard to find their way back.

If it's made from a certain type of stone, it can be used to help start fires. This reminds us to remember the past when life was harder, and how the tribal family all helped one another to survive—no disease, slavery, or pollution was present.

The biggest loss here is the song of the birds and animals.

Since European people began to arrive, they brought their own plants, birds, and animals, with them ruining our natural balance forever.

Four Sacred Medicines/Spiritual Weapons: Sage, Sweetgrass, Cedar, & Tobacco

Tobacco

Kinnickinnick is one of the very first gifts/medicines from the creator—it was pure, plain, and with no chemicals or poisons mixed into it. It's a direct line to the creator, ancestors, and spirit world; tobacco down, prayers up.

Tobacco is sacred and used for ceremonial, medicinal, and spiritual purposes. Gifting tobacco is a sign of respect, and is offered when asking for help, advice, guidance, or protection.

The smoke from the tobacco carries thoughts, prayers, and petitions to the spirit world. Tobacco can be smoked in a sacred pipe, the *chanupa,* in hand, or placed on the ground and in a sacred fire. It's used for cleansing and is sprinkled outside in the four corners of your home for protection. It is given as offerings and placed on graves.

Prayer ties and spiritual bundles are made with tobacco. Tobacco is always used first and is offered for everything and in every ceremony. It opens us up to the spirit world; the spirits love the sweet aroma of tobacco.

Sweetgrass

Sweetgrass is the hair of Mother Earth, is a gift from our creator. It's used for cleansing, smudging, purifying, and ceremonies. It attracts positive energies; it is sacred, powerful, and dispels negative energy.

It's used for healing, peace, and spiritual doings, and it's also left at graves and sacred sites. It has a beautiful aroma.

There are sweetgrass braids, incense, oils, soaps, and body butters made straight from American Indians.

Cedar

When cedar is lit and/or put in fire, it crackles; it's calling the attention of the spirits and our ancestors.

It's used for smudging, purifying, baths, teas, and healing, as well as for protection, dreams, and ceremonies.

Sage

Sage is harvested on tribal lands and exchanged through tribal people. We don't buy it from grocery stores or department stores, because it's fake, *not* the real deal, not from an American Indian's sacred ground.

Sage is used for smudging, cleansing, teas, healing, ceremonies, and the releasing or removal of negative energies. It is used to drive out evil influences and to ward off bad luck.

Don't make the tea and drink if you don't know how to, or have not been shown by an American Indian.

American Indians are troubled by the appropriation of sage and smudging. "Smudge" is not our word, nor our language. *Smudge* or *smudged* are consumers, new agers, and the beauty wellness industry's way of communicating this.

Growing up, I've heard a variety of terms in my family—rising smoke, cleansing, clearing, smoking, burning, smudging, and/or cleanse and clear.

Sage is medicine for many of our people, and by abusing it or misusing it, it is an insult and is disrespectful to our practices.

Sage Spray
For those who can't light sage, due to fire alarms activating, or you are on the go, here are a couple of different ways to make it.

Option #1

Things You'll Need:

- Blue Glass - Spray Bottle
- Grandmother Moon Water *(or Holy Water)*
- Sage Essential Oil *(50 drops, depending on the level of scent you like)*

Directions:

Put the items inside the spray bottle, and use.

Please note: Using the essential oil is for those who can't get their hands on actual sage, and/or can't keep to the other options of making sage spray.

Option #2

Things You'll Need:

- Blue Glass - Spray Bottle
- Sage Leaves
- Grandmother Moon Water *(or Holy Water)*
- Rubbing Alcohol *(a couple drops)*
- Cedar *(optional)*

Directions:

1. Put all the items in a jar with a lid, and when you feel like it's ready, strain it into the spray bottle.
2. You can put the spray bottle underneath Grandmother Moon for her medicine and energy, and all the wonderful things Grandmother Moon blesses with her light.

Sage, Cornmeal, & Tobacco Mix

Things You'll Need:

- Sage
- Cornmeal
- Tobacco
- Burning Bowl *(or Shell)*
- Birds of Prey Feathers *(optional)*

Directions:

1. Put the mix into a safe burning bowl (or shell) and light it.
2. Fan it out with the air from your hands, or feathers. (Don't blow it out with your breath, because you could be having a bad day, and your breath of unwanted energies will go onto the flame, and you don't want that.)
3. **Optional:* Use feathers to fan out the flame and/or for smudging. *Real birds of prey are used:* turkey feathers, eagle feathers, or hawk feathers that you can only get from an American Indian. (Feathers are given and/or traded; they are not bought. You also need to have a permit to carry these feathers. I, myself, have a permit.)

Please note: Fake feathers that are colored or spray-painted are bought from craft stores and department stores. These are not the real deal, so when you go out there purchasing yours, as I've seen it called inside "smudge kits," it's all fake. *Real* birds of prey feathers are medicine.

4. Go room-to-room, starting with the first floor and work your way up if you have multiple floors in your personal home or living space. (If not, it's okay.)
5. Open one window or door to let out the unwanted energies and/or unwanted spirit/s.
6. Open the closet doors and cabinets, and make sure you get the corners as well. When you clear the area or room, close the closet doors and cabinets behind you.
7. When done with this, seal it with sweetgrass.
8. Light the sweetgrass braid and shake (or blow out) the flame. You may have to light it a couple times to get it going, and blow on it to keep it lit.
9. Go room-to-room and open the closets and cabinets. When done, let the sweetgrass go out on its own, or smush it out gently.
1. Let the sage mixture go out on its own and discard the ashes outside on the steps or ground when they have cooled off. (Do this work twice in a row, if needed.)
10.

Lighting Sage

Things You'll Need:

- Sage
- Burning Bowl *(or Shell)*

Directions:

Light the sage, but, please, be careful. (Don't let the embers fall out of the burn-safe bowl, or shell, and don't discard the ashes in the trash.)

There are a few things to keep in mind…

- If you're having trouble lighting the sage,
- If the sage doesn't stay lit,
- If the sage is lit, and after you're going around, all of a sudden, *poof*—it flames up,

…this means that the area/space is no good, and/or spirit doesn't want you clearing them out.

If after cleansing, you notice that every area/room was smoky, but one particular area/room looks like there is no smoke, as if you didn't do anything, then you know that area had the most unwanted energy.

Cleansing Yourself

Things You'll Need:

- Sage *(or Sage Mix)*
- Burning Bowl *(or Shell)*

Directions:

1. Take the smoke of the sage (or sage mix), and cuff it in your hands.
2. Bring it over to these areas, going downwards head-to-feet:

I cleanse my *head* and *neck*.

I cleanse my *ears* and *eyes*.
I cleanse my *hands*.
I cleanse my *heart* and my *throat*.
I cleanse my *feet*.
May I, and this space, be cleansed and clear.

Moon Water

This working is meant to be completed on a full moon, as it's full for three nights and Grandmother Moon is at her highest.

Things You'll Need:

- Mason Jar
- Water
- Sage
- Cedar *(optional)*

Directions:

1. On the second night of the full moon, get a mason jar (or any jar with a lid), and cleanse it with sage.
2. Next, fill it with water.
3. Place the jar (or jars) in the windowsill. (If you're not able to put it outside, make sure it's where her light comes through in.)
4. Put the jar underneath her light on a bed of cedar to honor her. (If no cedar is present, it's okay.)
5. **Optional:* If you go to pick cedar, take tobacco with you, and give it to cedar as an offering and thanks. (Only take a few pieces, only what you need.)
6. Bring the jars out of her light before the sun rises. *Please note:* Don't let her water freeze, as in ice.
7. Grandmother Moon will turn that water into medicine. Drink it mindfully daily, and it will bring you healing and

> spiritual strength. When it's cloudy and stormy, and you can't see her light, just know that she is there, and her energy and powers are still there to do what she does best.

As women, we are connected to the moon; she gives us power. A woman's moon cycle that's synced to a full moon, these women are healers, magic makers, and wisdom keepers. It also allows for self-growth, creativity, development, and mentorship with other women.

They say, if you sleep outside, you'll sync your moon cycle with Grandmother Moon within one to two cycles.

The 7 Teachings

Each teaching is represented by an animal and shows respect for all living things.

1. *Love Eagle:* An undeniable force. Represents having and experiencing love. Fire symbol and the creator. Enjoying love through children.
2. *Respect Buffalo:* First and foremost, respect must be given in all life. Respect yourself and your body, and take care of yourself—self-care.
3. *Courage Bear:* Demonstrates the strength and courage we need in order to face our greatest enemy—ourselves. Represents resolutions from spiritual intervention, spiritual healing, and dealing with anger and pain.
4. *Honesty Sasquatch:* Is the law of the truth, reality. Meant to teach you survival, and how to be honest with yourself.
5. *Humility Wolf:* Family pack and survival. Everyone understands their individual role, and in our lives, humility becomes a factor in order to ask for guidance in a humbling way.

6. *Truth Turtle:* Law, principle, and time adapt to change without changing. The shell represents the thirteen moon cycles of the year.
7. *Wisdom Beaver:* Poison ruins water. It/you destroys oneself if you break the law of nature. Know the difference between wisdom and knowledge.

Spiritual Items

A bundle, or a special carrying bag and/or container box made of cedar wood for spiritual items that protect and give spiritual powers to its owner, can be any size and carried around your neck, waist, or shoulder.

There are a number of spiritual items carried, including a spirit. It's all spiritual value to the bundle's owner and is meant just for them.

These items are sacred, precious, holy, and are kept a secret by the owner. Bundles possess powers for protection, healing, good luck, and good hunting. Sometimes, the bundles are handed down from generation-to-generation to one chosen person, or buried with the owner.

To receive these items and bundle, or to be the carrier and to have such a bag or special box, how it's carved, sewn, and all put together is done through visions.

Like we mentioned in the previous chapter briefly, a vision quest is a rite of passage, a personal sacrifice.

You go to an isolated location for about a week. This is to make contact with spiritual forces of all kinds.

During this time, a guardian spirit will make their appearance in a vision or dream, and some items will represent their guardian spirit. These bundles can be carried for oneself and for others, and the owner of the medicine bundle can carry that for both.

Nowadays the misuse of information and the abuse of our ceremonies and medicine bundles has become worldwide at stores, fairs, and for groups of non-indigenous people. Fake medicine bundles, bags, and containers are found at stores and other places as mentioned above.

How do you know who made them? What material was used? How many hands and energy has touched it before walking to the register? Who appointed you as carrier?

There is a process from deep inside and certain spiritually deep elders. As I mentioned before, we don't like, *nor* want to be called *shamans. Medicine man/woman, spiritual advisor,* or *spiritualist* is a respectful way to phrase this.

There are many lies portrayed by so many walking around saying that they carry this by a non-Native American, and they only know three things, but half of those three things are wrong.

You don't *pay* to become one, and you don't find an ad online or in the newspaper. Medicine men/women don't advertise themselves online or verbally, or walk around handing out business cards. We carry ourselves in a sacred way always.

When seeking out spiritual counsel, there are a number of ways that people reach out.

- Calling or emailing the tribal office
- Word-of-mouth
- Asking if they can speak to a medicine man/woman directly

Their contact info is not given out without permission first.

We would hear what the person is seeking us out for, and we would speak to them if after a little thought and prayer, we received the permission of our spirits.

When you meet with a *spiritual advisor* or a *medicine man/woman,* remember to sit still, listen, and always give a gift or offering of tobacco, fruit, a blanket, and/or other herbs.

Medicine men/women have different abilities to help someone, but we all may not have those with veteran and military war spirits.

My niece had a visitor in her dream —my father. He told her exactly what needed to be done for one of my military sons. She contacted me; then, she contacted a friend to make the connection to whom only works with war spirits. My niece and I sent boxes of gifts and offerings to both parties. The medicine man asked for me to call him, and I did. Now, we are good friends.

He told me what he was going to do and make, and the spirits agreed.

There are weeks of ceremonies and placing items on ancestors' and war spirits' spaces. Some things are made and given to my son (for life), and a spirit is named and given to him (for life). We, as in my son, myself, and the medicine man, feed this spirit, especially when my son can't, because of certain areas and military duties.

The Day-to-Day Life of Traditional Medicine Work

Prayer

We pray for others before praying for ourselves, but if you start out praying for yourself, make that day of praying just for you and give thanks. Humble yourself and practice patience; never ask the creator for patience—this is the golden rule.

You can ask for impatience to be taken away, but asking flat out for patience, it will turn bad.

When we pray, we must make sure that it comes from the heart, and that we give thanks after each prayer.

Spirit plates are put out for our ancestors one- to three-times daily. I personally put out spirit plates for breakfast and dinner. Kinnickinnick is also placed out by the plates.

Incense or herbs are burned, and smudging ceremonies or spray cleansing is done. Also, food is placed out for the wildlife and spirit animals as well.

Making Medicines

This is a routine not just when you think it's needed. Non-indigenous trendy ways nowadays are using fake feathers, and telling you that you have to only go underneath the moon with *this* and *that* at certain times and days.

"You should *smudge* like this," and using the word *smudge.*

I hear, "Oh, I had a dream that I am destined to be a healer. My past life *this*...my past life *that.* I'm Native...I have no proof, but I heard we have something, so I'm gonna go host a spiritual retreat and charge money and give false teachings, filling candles and making up some sort of an item and calling it 'medicine'."

Don't be this person.

There are many things that I cannot mention, but I want to make it clear that as the clan mother of the tribe, I keep these things and make them precious. Just because you learn a few things doesn't mean that you should be teaching others. If you do this, you are one of the most, for a lack of better words, undesiring breathing individuals that could be reading this book. To be so disrespectful is unacceptable, intolerable, and at a certain point, we have to put our foot down.

Those Who are Chosen for this Path

Those traditionally gifted to provide these workings are spiritual leaders/healers and medicine men/women.

When I was 4-5 years old, my father who was the chief of our tribe and a powerful medicine man, healer, and seer—a "legend" they called him worldwide—he beaded a dead rattlesnake's full body into the loom, making a belt.

Now, some would say, "Oh, the nerves of animals/reptiles move after it dies." This wasn't the case. The rattlesnake was dead days before being beaded into the loom.

Days later, that rattlesnake's head swelled up in the belt. The neighbor who was a teacher thought it was cool and wanted to show the kids in his class.

He had the belt on his dining room table, and his German Shepard was going crazy, growling and barking at the belt because it was shaking.

The dog got ahold of it, chewed it up, and tore it apart to the point that there was nothing left but the loom.

The dog died suddenly, and the neighbor's wife suddenly became ill and died too. The neighbors' lives went downhill fast; there was nothing but bad luck since that day.

The neighbor also died himself. All three died in that house.

One day, I was on our living room floor playing when a non-rattlesnake slithered close by my leg and knee, playing with me. My father walked over and grabbed the snake. Till this day, during a certain season in the year, every year, I have to rub snake oil on an area that likes to act up in different ways.

My father told my sister, speaking about me, "That snake that came to her was in her hands and played with her. Who are we to question the spirit world?"

Children can see with their innocent eyes what we're unable to. My sister told me, "You've attracted it."

We are looked upon as the chosen ones by the elders watching and seeing who has encountered those different gifted abilities.

Note: Please, stay away from snake medicine; don't dabble into something you have no idea about. You can kill someone just by trying to heal them and doing good by it. Snake medicine is nothing to mess around with. Don't keep snake pieces around trying to connect. *Danger*...stay away!

CHAPTER 4
The Cycle of Turtle Island

A turtle's back represents the 13 moons and 28-day cycle.

Moon Calendar

- *January:* Midwinter, Wolf
- *February:* Snow
- *March:* Maple Syrup
- *April:* Thunder Season, the Pink Moon
- *May:* Seed Season, Planting Seeds
- *June:* Strawberry, Thanksgiving
- *July:* Beans, Green Beans
- *August:* Green Corn
- *September:* Harvest
- *October:* Food Storing
- *November:* Hunting, Blue
- *December:* Long Nights, Resting

There are few different names associated with the moon. The waters are powered by Grandmother Moon. Water is life; water is sacred.

Grandmother Moon, and grandmothers in general, power us as well. Women are very sacred, as well as children. When women are on their moon time, we must refrain from making medicines and food, as we are very powerful.

Each moon cycle, we ask Grandmother Moon for release, cleansing, renewal, guidance, healing, direction, and wisdom. Always remember, we release, cleanse, and renew from the powers of her light.

A lot of us who are very well connected to Grandmother Moon do other spiritual doings during this time.

Celebrations and ceremonies come with each moon month. Tribes have a private celebration of thanks and honoring of the moons: Harvesting, Hunting, Strawberry, etc.

Holy Days We Celebrate

During the month of October, our tribe, which comes from the Black Bear Clan, we honor the bear before hibernation. We have a celebration with a ceremony, drumming, singing, and dancing. We have a sacred fire and gather around the fire and proceed with ceremony.

Taking a piece of the foods the bear eats, which are nuts, fish, and berries, we also place a spirit plate out for the bears.

When around the fire, we take our tobacco and give thanks and honor to the black bear and our ancestors. We say prayers for the bear's hibernation, bear medicine, and our connection to the bear. Bear root is also placed out for the bears to eat when they come out of hibernation in order to cleanse their digestive system. We also use bear root in ceremonies for healing properties.

During September/October, it is harvesting time. We are gathering herbs from the lands/woods; we gather berries and medicines, and clean, dry, and bag them; freeze and/or jar them for wintertime, when nothing is available on the land, as winter closes everything down for a long sleep.

March is all about maple syrup! We plug those maple trees for the syrup to drain and be bottled up. We tell stories and have lots of syrup for families to take home, and we feast and do a rattle dance.

In May, we start planting seeds for new herbs, vegetables, fruits, or more is added to what is already on the land.

June holds our Strawberry and Thanksgiving ceremonies. This means that we collect and eat strawberries and drink tea. Some tribes even go on a berry fast.

In July and August, the same celebrations as mentioned above are held, just for a different food. We offer these foods to our ancestors, the creator, and the Great Spirit, thanking them and Mother Earth for providing us with these foods, blessings, and new beginnings.

CLOSING PRAYER

Honorable ancestors, known and unknown, the creator, and our Mother Earth, may you guide me to work the land and care for the land with love and grace. May I place my healing hands into the soil with a good positive aura and energy into the land of earth, so it may heal . Aho

Made in the USA
Columbia, SC
22 April 2025